A DK PUBLISHING BOOK

Project Editor Caroline Bingham
Art Editor Mike Buckley

US Editor Camela Decaire
Deputy Managing Editor Mary Ling
Senior Art Editor Jane Horne

Production David Hyde
Picture Research Ingrid Nilsson

**Photography, at risk to life
and limb, by** Frank Greenaway
and Kim Taylor

Additional photography by Karl Shone
and Jerry Young

First American Edition 1996
2 4 6 8 10 9 7 5 3 1

Published in the United States by
DK Publishing, Inc.,
95 Madison Avenue,
New York, New York 10016
http://www.dk.com

Published in Great Britain by Dorling Kindersley Limited.

Distributed by Houghton Mifflin Company, Boston.

A CIP catalog record for this book
is available from the Library of Congress.

ISBN: 0-7894-1029-X

Color reproduction by Colourscan
Printed in Italy by L.E.G.O.

The publisher would like to thank the following
for their kind permission to reproduce their photographs:

t top, b bottom, l left, r right, c center.

Bruce Coleman/Jan Taylor (Greedy Invaders: tl)/Kim Taylor
(Dirty Visitors: tr/Chompers: tc); Oxford Scientific Films/Mike Birkhead
(Chompers: tl)/Tim Shepherd (Bloodsuckers: tr); Premaphotos
(Greedy Invaders: cl, br).

Open Wide!

Bloodsuckers

A Big Appetite

Good Grub

The Really
FEARSOME
BLOOD-LOVING
VAMPIRE
BAT

Greedy Invaders

AND OTHER CREATURES WITH
STRANGE EATING HABITS

THERESA GREENAWAY

Dirty Visitors

Chompers

Night Fright

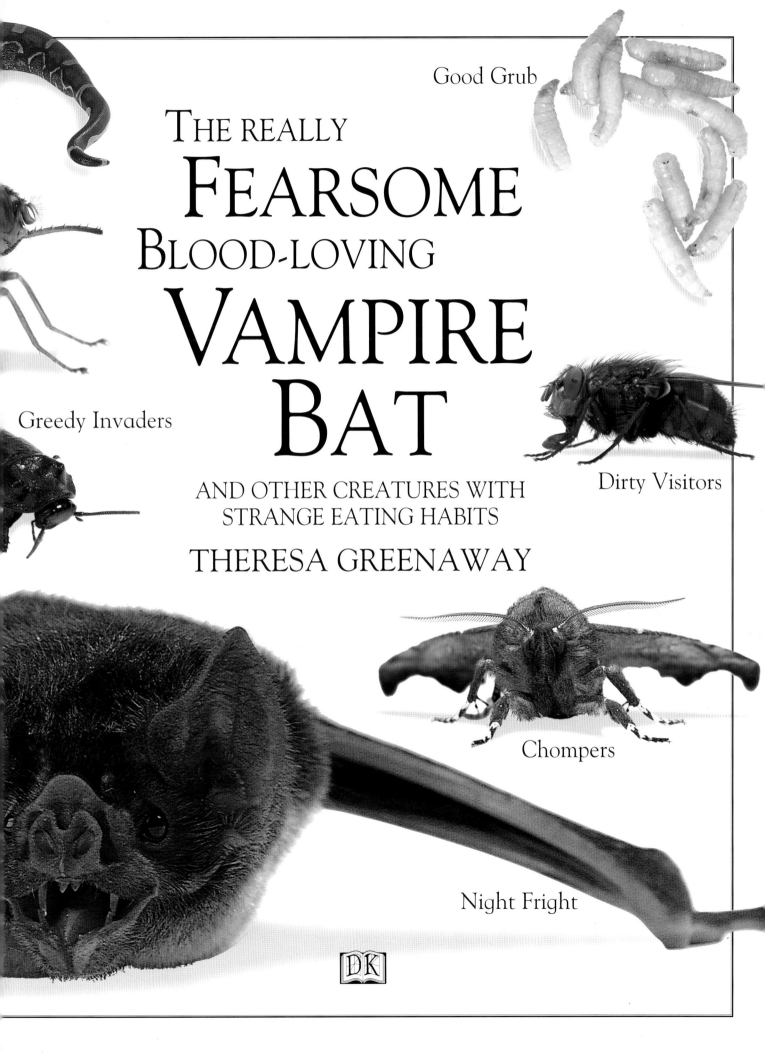

DK

NIGHT FRIGHT

They come out to fly only at night and drink blood to stay alive – no wonder people think bats are scary! In fact, only one kind of bat drinks blood. Most eat insects.

Franquet's fruit bat

Only vampire bats feed on blood. Other bats eat insects, animals, fruit, or nectar.

Naked-backed bat

A vampire bat with a full tummy will vomit up blood to feed a hungry relative.

Vampire bat

A Daubenton's bat swoops down low over a lake, catching insects from the surface of the water in its teeth.

Insect-eating bats can eat up to half their own body weight in a single night.

Fruit bats crush fruits in their mouths and swallow the juice. They spit out the seeds and skins.

Daubenton's bat

Long-eared bats have sharp teeth. They bite off moths' wings, then crunch up everything else.

Long-eared bat

A vampire bat slices into skin with razor-sharp front teeth. Its saliva stops blood from clotting, so it flows and flows as long as the vampire laps it up.

This spear-nosed bat's favorite meal is some juicy fruit and a tasty insect.

Spear-nosed bat

GREEDY INVADERS

Only a few of the 4,000 or so species of cockroaches are pests, but they'll eat just about anything – from crumbs and grease to paper and old shoes. The rest live harmlessly in the wild.

Cockroaches from Australia

Cockroaches long, sensitive antennae can sense a movement on the ground of less than one millionth of an inch. Move – and they'll know that you're there!

Cockroach from Madagascar

Suriname cockroach

Young cockroaches look just like adults, but they are smaller and wingless. Their wings appear at about six months.

Many cockroaches have stink glands. These produce a disgusting smell if the insects feel threatened.

Cockroaches are often found in grubby places – such as a dirty kitchen with lots of food!

American cockroach

One pair of cockroaches can result in 100,000 a year later.

Cockroaches deposit their eggs in an egg purse attached to their abdomen. Each purse has two neat rows of eggs inside.

Female cockroach with egg purse

Many cockroaches forage for food on forest floors.

Because cockroaches are flat in shape, they are really good at hiding in narrow crevices.

Cockroach from South America

Hissing cockroach from Central America

If this cockroach is threatened, it makes a sudden hiss to startle its attacker.

DIRTY VISITORS

Flies can ruin any picnic! They crawl over dirt and then onto food, spreading germs that can make people sick.

There are more than 85,000 different kinds of flies.

Dung flies love to lay their eggs in fresh, moist cowpats. When the eggs hatch, the grubs dig in to their first meal – rotting dung.

Dung fly

For lunch, a bluebottle flits between rotting meat, a pile of

Dirt and germs stick to hairs all over a fly's body and legs. Flies never wash!

House flies

A robber fly sucks the juices out of its prey.

Robber fly eating a lacewing fly

Robber flies catch insects with their hairy legs. Then, piercing mouthparts inject venom.

dung, and your sandwich – unless you watch out!

Bluebottles dribble spit onto food to dissolve it, then mop up the juice.

Bluebottle fly

BLOODSUCKERS

A bite from one of these insects is often painful and can itch for days. Worse still, while they are filling up with your blood, some may infect you with diseases.

Only female mosquitoes drink blood – and it's not always human blood.

Female mosquito

This female mosquito prefers the blood of birds.

Most insects lay eggs, but a female tsetse produces live young – just one at a time!

A tsetse fly can drink three times its own weight in blood in one

Blood-filled male tsetse fly

Bloodsucking mosquito

Pregnant tsetse fly

A mosquito's spit can spread a disease called malaria, causing chills and fever.

gulp! This one is so full it can hardly fly.

Tsetse fly

Bloodsucking insects have stretchy stomachs, but when they're hungry, you can barely see them. This fly needs a meal!

Tsetse flies carry an organism that can cause a fatal sleeping sickness that affects both people and animals.

A BIG APPETITE

With their long legs and biting mouthparts, these insects have no trouble grasping food to eat. And they love to eat, and eat, and eat...

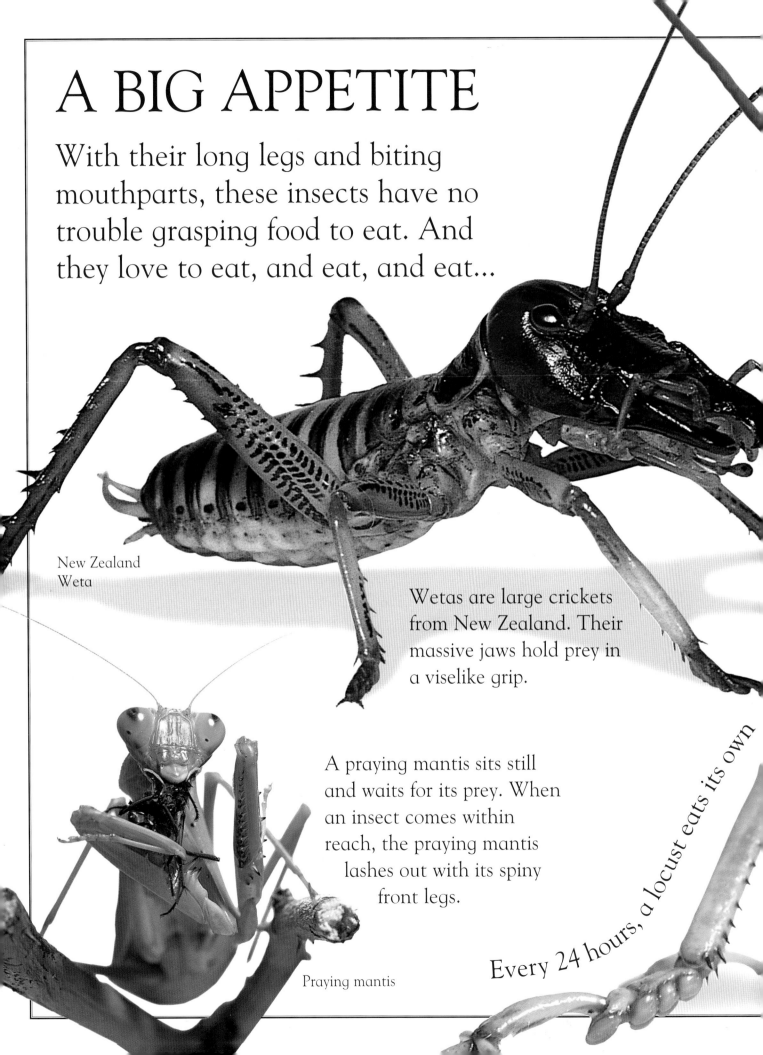

New Zealand Weta

Wetas are large crickets from New Zealand. Their massive jaws hold prey in a viselike grip.

A praying mantis sits still and waits for its prey. When an insect comes within reach, the praying mantis lashes out with its spiny front legs.

Praying mantis

Every 24 hours, a locust eats its own

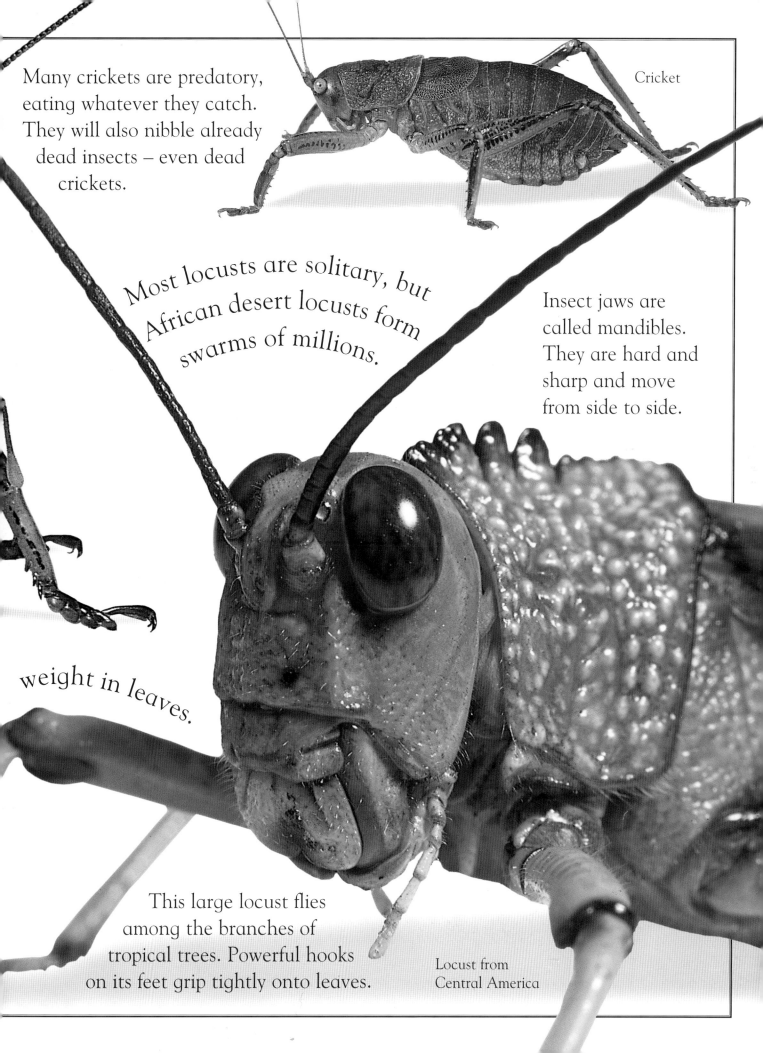

Many crickets are predatory,
eating whatever they catch.
They will also nibble already
dead insects – even dead
crickets.

Cricket

Most locusts are solitary, but
African desert locusts form
swarms of millions.

Insect jaws are
called mandibles.
They are hard and
sharp and move
from side to side.

weight in leaves.

This large locust flies
among the branches of
tropical trees. Powerful hooks
on its feet grip tightly onto leaves.

Locust from
Central America

CHOMPERS

Clothes moths love to eat
sweaters, but most moths
have harmless eating habits.
Some don't eat at all!

Clothes moths

Some moths use their feet to "taste."

Moths feed on the
sugary nectar made by
flowers. Hawk-moths like
honeysuckle nectar.

Hawk-moth

A moth's tongue
is a long, thin tube
called a proboscis. It
is used like a straw.

This male moth has huge, feathery antennae...

Tau Emperor moth

Moths' wings are covered with minute,
powdery scales. Some moths also have
special scent scales, but only other
moths can smell them.

Elephant hawk-moth

that can pick up the scent of a female moth even if she is a long way off.

Polyphemus moth

There are about 153,000 kinds of moths, and some don't eat. Those that don't get energy from the food they ate as caterpillars.

When a moth is not feeding, its strawlike proboscis coils up under its head.

Brimstone moth

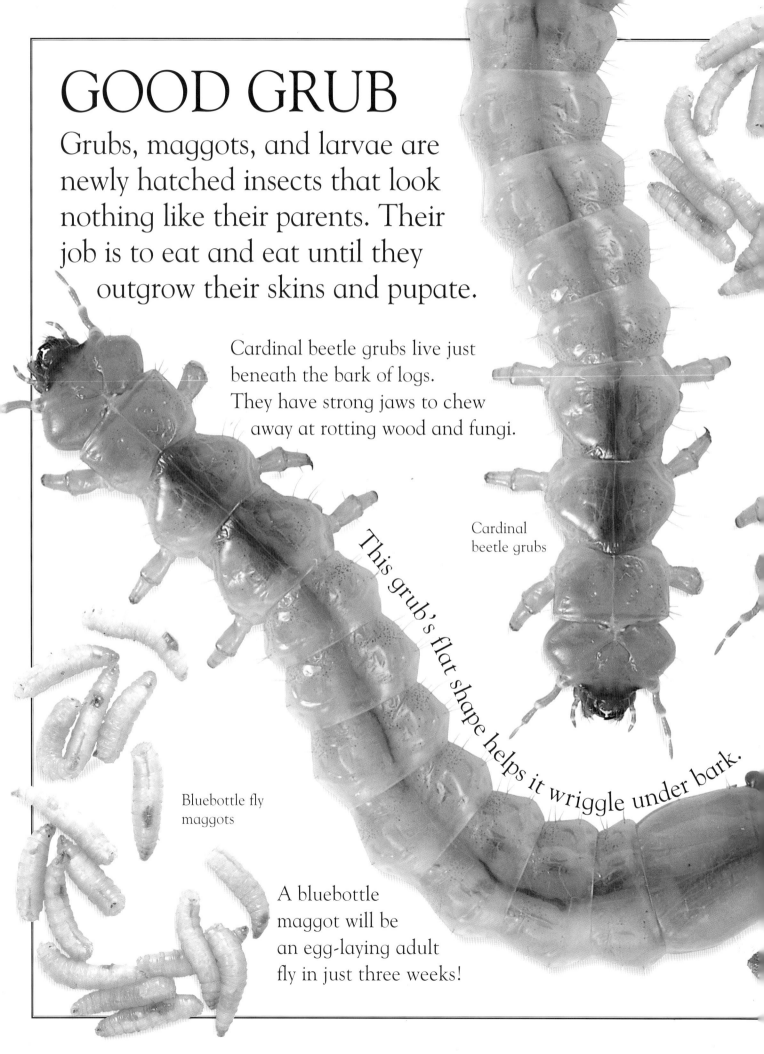

GOOD GRUB

Grubs, maggots, and larvae are newly hatched insects that look nothing like their parents. Their job is to eat and eat until they outgrow their skins and pupate.

Cardinal beetle grubs live just beneath the bark of logs. They have strong jaws to chew away at rotting wood and fungi.

Cardinal beetle grubs

This grub's flat shape helps it wriggle under bark.

Bluebottle fly maggots

A bluebottle maggot will be an egg-laying adult fly in just three weeks!

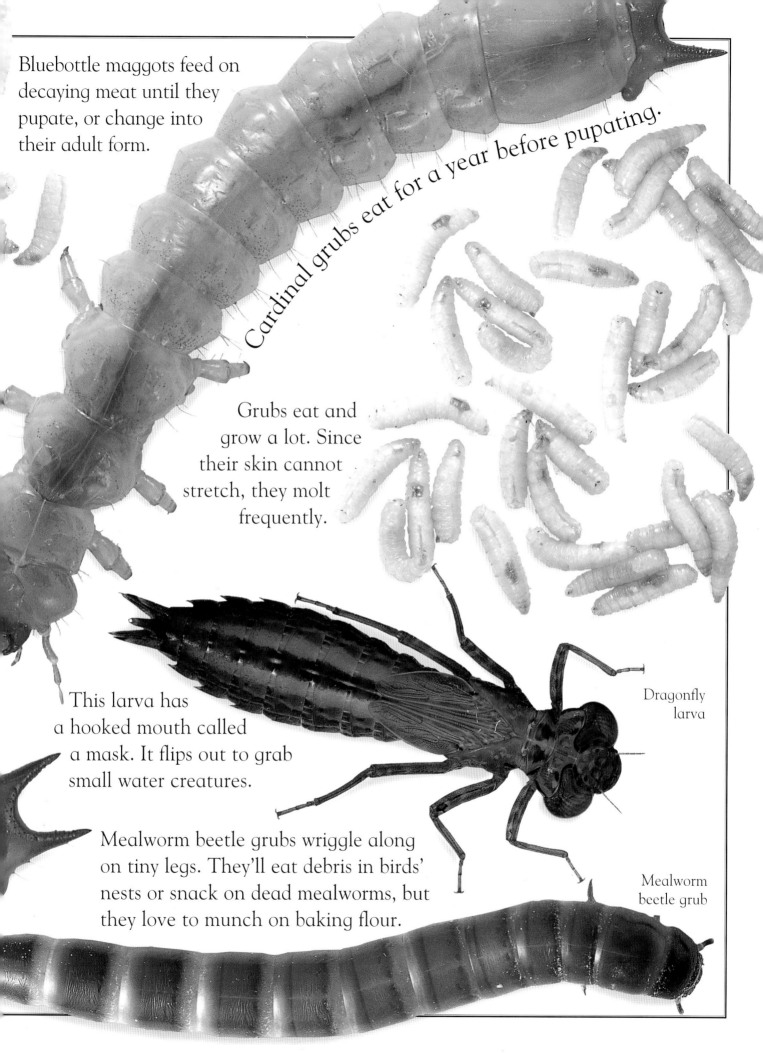

Bluebottle maggots feed on decaying meat until they pupate, or change into their adult form.

Cardinal grubs eat for a year before pupating.

Grubs eat and grow a lot. Since their skin cannot stretch, they molt frequently.

This larva has a hooked mouth called a mask. It flips out to grab small water creatures.

Dragonfly larva

Mealworm beetle grubs wriggle along on tiny legs. They'll eat debris in birds' nests or snack on dead mealworms, but they love to munch on baking flour.

Mealworm beetle grub

OPEN WIDE!

Different snakes eat different foods, from tiny eggs to big, fat goats. But all snakes either paralyze or kill their victim before they start to swallow...

Python with rat

A snake is basically one stretchy stomach, with a head at

Snakes cannot chew – they swallow prey whole.

A snake has to kill its prey quickly. This is not just to stop it from escaping, but to prevent the snake from being injured while swallowing.

Puff-adder

Constrictors, such as pythons, squeeze their prey until it suffocates.

Some snakes can swallow food twice the size of their heads!

Common lancehead

one end and a tail at the other.

Venomous snakes, such as the lancehead, inject lethal poisons into their prey with long, pointed fangs.

This Californian king snake will gobble up anything – even other poisonous snakes if it has the chance!

Their mouths open wider and wider to fit around almost anything.

Californian mountain king snake